GOOD NEWS
OF GREAT JOY

ADVENT
REFLECTIONS
ON THE SONGS
OF LUKE

MAX O. VINCENT

UPPER
ROOM BOOKS®
NASHVILLE

Cover design: Bruce Gore
Cover imagery: iStock by Getty Images
Typesetting and interior design: PerfecType, Nashville, TN

ISBN: 978-0-8358-1970-1
Mobi ISBN: 978-0-8358-1971-8
Epub ISBN: 978-0-8358-1972-5

For John and Pat
In memoriam

Sing and make music from
your heart to the Lord.
—Ephesians 5:19, NIV

CONTENTS

CONTENTS

ACKNOWLEDGMENTS

Working with Upper Room Books makes writing fun; it also makes my writing better. This book would not be possible without the encouragement and insight of their staff. Thanks once again to Joanna Bradley Kennedy, Editorial Director, for entering a conversation about the idea of this book and helping form my thoughts into a coherent proposal. Amy Barham is a patient editor who worked hard to clarify my thinking and writing.

During Advent of 2019, a group at St. James United Methodist Church in Atlanta, where I am privileged to serve as one of the pastors, was kind enough to participate in a weekly Sunday night study of the canticles in Luke 1–2. This group endured very rough drafts of the material presented in this book. Their enthusiastic participation helped me clarify some of my thoughts about how important these canticles can be in our lives today. From the beginning, I wanted this to be a study that involved the arts to illustrate and highlight the biblical texts. This group willingly searched out and shared their responses to different musical settings of these texts and paintings of the characters who sing these biblical songs.

Other friends and colleagues read parts of this book or listened to ideas. Reverend Beth Brown Shugart used an early version of this material with a study group at Duluth UMC in December of 2020. This book is better thanks to the insights, questions, and suggestions of all of these groups; any errors remaining are my responsibility.

Without the support of my wife, Kristen, and our son, Matthew, I would not have completed this work. The rewriting and editing occurred during the COVID-19 epidemic of 2020. Most of that time, our family was confined together in our apartment. They listened, not always by choice, to a lot of Christmas music and multiple performances of each canticle in June, July, and August. Matthew and Kristen made gracious room for Mary, Zechariah, Simeon, and a host of angels in our discussions and let these intruders demand a good deal of my time and attention. Kristen and Matthew, thank you for your gracious hospitality.

I dedicate the book to the memory of my parents. Pat and John first taught me the joy of music and singing. I have forgotten many things they tried to teach me across the years, but this lesson continues to nourish my life. Thanks, Mom and Dad.

INTRODUCTION

Music is integral to Christmas. Even people who do not sing at other times of the year find it difficult to refrain from caroling and joining Christmas hymns. Ebenezer Scrooge at the beginning of *A Christmas Carol* may be the caricature exception that proves the ubiquity of joyfully singing at Christmas. As Christmas Eve descends, Scrooge hears a voice at his keyhole. But "at the first sound of—'God bless you, merry gentleman! May nothing you dismay!'" Scrooge jumps up with his ruler as if to attack the caroler.[1]

Most of us thrill to the first sounds of Christmas songs played in stores or over the radio. For us, these sounds build an anticipation for Christmas. The tones of Christmas strike resonant chords in our emotions, evoking visceral responses. They recall memories and create expectations. We start to hum the tunes and sing the words. Our bodies move to the cadence of the carols. Their rhythms move us through our preparations and celebration of Christmas. Music is vital to this season.

For many, the Christmas season begins with Black Friday sales and lasts until December 25. But according to the church calendar, Advent begins four Sundays before Christmas, and Christmas is a season of twelve days, beginning December 25. Advent and Christmas are distinct seasons, but they are related.

The word *advent* derives from the Latin word *adventus,* meaning "coming." This season celebrates the appearance of God in Jesus Christ, God's presence with us today through Word and Spirit, and God's future coming to us in the fullness of time. Christmas is a twelve-day season of thanksgiving for God's coming to us at a particular moment in human flesh through Jesus of Nazareth. Advent is more than preparation for Christmas. It calls us to look for signs of God's presence today and creates a longing for God's full presence in the future.

Advent and Christmas are both musically rich seasons. Many churches struggle each year, trying to decide the proper time to start singing Christmas carols versus Advent hymns. Do we lose the mystery of God's current presence and the wonder at God's return to us if we jump too early to Christmas carols? However, Christmas music is some of the most beautiful music we have. If we limit this music to just the twelve days of Christmas, it hardly seems fair. Though, we occasionally neglect some beautiful Advent hymns by rushing too soon to Christmas carols.

The rhythms of Christmas music move our bodies, while the poetry of the lyrics captures our minds and hearts. Plus, carols are easy to sing—not only because they are so well known, which is often true, but also because carols are simple, rhythmic, joyful songs. Carols are less complicated than much other choral music, so they are easy to learn and fun to sing, especially in groups. From the twelfth-century

French carol "The Friendly Beasts" through the Polish carol "Infant Holy, Infant Lowly" to the sixteenth-century English carol "God Rest Ye Merry, Gentlemen," carols are some of our best-loved music.

But the music of Christmas did not begin with the many carols by unknown composers, the first half of Handel's *Messiah*, or Charles Wesley's "Hark! The Herald Angels Sing." It began with the singing of angels outside of Bethlehem. The angels sing in the idiom of Jewish piety. Their song captures significant themes of the Old Testament and gives us the means to sing the faith into the future. Their rhythmic chorus tunes our lives to live in light of God's promises. Christianity learned from Judaism the value of singing hymns to sustain the faith. Luke records three other songs of praise in his opening chapters before and after the angels sing. These songs welcome the birth of Jesus as the fulfillment of God's promises.

We call the four songs at the beginning of Luke *canticles*. *Canticle* comes from another Latin word, *canticulum*, meaning "little song." We use this term to describe hymns in the Bible located outside the book of Psalms. The four canticles in Luke 1–2 entered the church's regular worship early and are still in common use today. In some traditions of the church, these canticles are daily prayers. As with Christmas carols, it's hard not to join in singing these songs (many of the prayer settings call for singing or chanting these texts). The traditional names for these canticles come from the first words of their texts in the Latin translation of the Bible. The four canticles are the *Magnificat* (Luke 1:46-55), the *Benedictus* (Luke 1:68-79), the *Gloria in Excelsis* (Luke 2:14), and the *Nunc Dimittis* (Luke 2:29-32).

These songs interrupt the narrative flow of Luke's story of the birth of Jesus. Each occurs after some announcement of God's coming into the lives of the biblical characters. The characters hear this decree of divine presence as a message of great comfort, which leads to their joyous singing.

The canticles appear before, at, and after the birth of Jesus. Like Advent, they give thanks for the past, celebrate the present, and long for God's future presence. Yet the songs all appear in the Christmas story. It seems the early church struggled with the distinction between Advent hymns and Christmas carols as well. In the biblical context, we seem more likely to hear Advent hymns in the midst of Christmas, as if to remind us that God does not stop coming to us after the birth of Jesus.

By interrupting the flow of the story, these songs make us slow down and consider the deeper meaning of what is going on in the narrative. These meditations invite us to ponder the significance of these stories, to seek connections to earlier scriptures, and to ask how these words intersect with our lives today. They also remind us of God's faithfulness to previous generations, encourage us to look for signs of God's presence today, and create a joyful response within us to this good news of God's coming to us.

Each canticle will be the focus of one section of this book. The canticles begin with four different verbs describing different ways to praise God: *magnify*, *bless*, *glorify*, and *depart in peace*. Each section of the book starts with an essay introducing the respective verb of praise for the given canticle. The remainder of each section has readings about the singer, the song, and the spirituality cultivated within us today by continuing to use these ancient songs of the faith. The written material puts the song in context to aid our meditation on the text. Each reading ends with suggested practices to help us explore different ways to meditate on and with the canticle. There are practices in each section suggesting the use of music and art, encouraging a multisensory experience of each canticle.

The book is a set of meditations for the season of Advent. There are six readings in each section for a total of twenty-four daily readings, excluding the introduction and conclusion. If you are using the book in personal study, you might study one reading a day during December, leading up to Christmas. If you are using this book as part of a group study, you may want to focus on one section each week. There is a brief leader's guide at the back of the book with suggestions for running a weekly group study. Whatever way you choose to engage this material, my prayer is that through this study, you will hear the voices of angels celebrating God's presence in your life and find the strength to add your voice to that joyful chorus.

Practice

- Read the first two chapters of the Gospel of Luke. What are some of your favorite Advent or Christmas songs?

SECTION ONE

Mary's Song

❧

The *Magnificat*: Luke 1:46-55

Context: Luke 1:26-45, 56

Magnifying the Lord

"My soul magnifies the Lord."
—LUKE 1:46

When I was six years old, my parents gave me a stamp-collecting kit and a coin-collecting kit for Christmas. Both were world collections. I learned about other countries mainly by sorting those collections. I would find a stamp or coin, identify the country it was from, see if I could locate the country on a map, and then place it on the correct page of the respective album. My older brothers and sisters were glad that sorting these stamps and coins kept me occupied for hours. My parents were happy that I was learning a lot of geography. I mostly enjoyed the plastic magnifying glasses that came with each kit.

I had never worked with a magnifying glass before. I was amazed at how this little tool could enhance my vision, helping me read and identify markings and letters that I could hardly see with my unaided eyes. It took me one week to convince my father that I needed a real glass one with a larger magnifier to be a bona fide collector. I was fascinated with magnification.

These coin and stamp collections taught me the value of focusing, of examining something for more than what we catch in a momentary glance. I learned that sometimes we need tools to enhance our vision. But most importantly, these collections created a sense of excitement, anticipation, and wonder at perceiving more than what was visible at first sight.

At the end of each school day, my joy grew at the thought of coming home to learn new details of another coin or stamp. I rushed off the school bus, ran to my room, and opened my collections. With my real magnifying glass in hand, I would get lost in the joy of discovery.

Advent builds similar excitement in our lives. Advent is a strange mixture of the already and the not yet. There is a remembrance of the first coming of Christ at Christmas, the already. There is also an anticipation of the day when we will be fully present with Christ, the future coming of Christ into our midst, the not yet. But Advent also invites us to the surprising discovery of Christ among us now, a revelation that sometimes takes intense focus. This focus feels like taking up a magnifying glass only to learn what was always right in front of us.

The *Magnificat* displays this kind of surprise over a new worldview opening for us when we see signs of God at work in our midst, even within us today. Mary's song grows out of her meditation on God's coming to her. Singing her song heightens our awareness of God with us in the here and now. Through her singing, Mary invites us to magnify our perception of what God has done, will do, and is doing in us.

Mary's song is like quilt work, stitching together strands of praise from Israel's heritage into a new statement of the faith. Like a folk singer versed in the traditional songs of her people, she sings the old story of God's surprising presence in a new day. Mary grew up singing the psalms and canticles of the Old Testament. The *Magnificat* is born from a long gestation period of pondering how the songs of her faith could give voice to her wonder at God's work in her.

Practice

- Read Luke 1:26-56. The *Magnificat* (see Luke 1:46-55) has often been used at evening prayers in the Western church. Try reciting this text each evening as you work through this section. As you speak and meditate on the words, what events from the day come to mind? Where have you noticed God's presence throughout the day?

The Perplexed Singer

L uke introduces Mary in the middle of another story. It is the story of the birth of John the Baptist. John's father, Zechariah, is a priest serving in the Temple when the angel Gabriel appears to tell him that he and his wife, Elizabeth, will have a son. It is in the sixth month of this story about Elizabeth's pregnancy that the angel appears to Mary. Gabriel's visitation to Mary unsettles her. The interruption is so jarring that Luke describes Mary as "perplexed" (1:29).

Mary's puzzlement occurs in response to Gabriel's announcement that God is present with her. Whereas Zechariah is a priest serving in the Temple in Jerusalem when Gabriel visits him, Mary is a young woman in an obscure village at the time of her visitation. We often go to worship or take a retreat hoping to encounter God. We may not be expecting a personal visit from an angel as Zechariah receives. Still, most of us, hoping to hear from God, journey to a particular place, a sanctuary or holy spot, thinking we are more likely to hear from God away from our usual surroundings. We seldom think about experiencing God in our daily living and location. Encounters with God in the ordinary upset our routine and reorder our lives; they surprise and perplex us.

Mary is in her hometown, Nazareth, when the angel finds her. The Bible does not mention Nazareth before the story of Jesus. No great revelations or angel visits occur there in the Old Testament. We do not even know the town's origins. Luke says it's someplace in the region of Galilee. Nazareth does not sound like the most likely place for an encounter with God. We know the town today because Mary's son, Jesus, grew up here.

Luke does not say where Mary is in Nazareth when Gabriel finds her. If we visited Nazareth today, we would find two churches built to commemorate this encounter. The Greek Orthodox Church covers the old town well, where one legend says the Annunciation occurred. Another tradition says this took place in her home, so the Roman Catholic Church is atop the remains of an ancient house thought to be Mary's home. Perhaps she was praying in the synagogue. All we know from scripture is God sent Gabriel to find Mary somewhere in this obscure village.

Luke makes no mention of Mary's family, much less the location of her home. Besides being from Nazareth, we know that she is engaged to a guy named Joseph. Joseph, at least, is from the family of David. That connection to King David is the most prestigious thing about this story so far. Well, except for the fact that an angel is coming to speak to this young woman. Though her visitation by Gabriel occurs in this obscure village, his message makes this visitation even more dramatic than Zechariah's visitation in the Temple.

It's safe to assume Mary had no previous angel sight-ings. Luke does not comment on her response to the angel's presence but to the angel's greeting, "The Lord is with you" (1:28). The focus is on the words. Gabriel does not tell her that she needs to go somewhere to find God or that she has to pray so often for so many days to experience God. The angel simply proclaims God's presence in Mary's life, even in Nazareth. This angelic salutation perplexes Mary, and she ponders these words.

The word translated "perplexed," *diatarasso*, is only used at this point in the Bible. It means more than confu-sion or uncertainty. The word speaks of an intense inner back and forth between emotions. That Mary might have extreme emotional responses is understandable. First of all, she is seeing and talking with an angel. Second, the angel speaks of God's high favor of Mary and that God is with her. Well might Mary toss about between fear and joy, sur-prise and wonder. The book of Hebrews could be describ-ing Mary when it says, "It is a fearful thing to fall into the hands of the living God" (10:31). The angel says this living God is already with Mary. She does not have to go some-where to find him. She is not too ordinary or insignificant for God to take notice of her. God is with her in Nazareth of all places. Is it any wonder she is perplexed?

Practice

- The Annunciation to Mary is a favorite theme in works of art. Search for various images from different cen-turies. Choose some favorite depictions of this scene.

Compare them. Study the images to see what emotions are expressed. Is Mary shocked? surprised? afraid? serene? What image best depicts how you would have responded to this angelic greeting?

Pondering with Mary

Thankfully, Mary is not just perplexed. She stays and ponders these words of Gabriel: "She was much perplexed by his words and pondered what sort of greeting this might be" (Luke 1:29). She could have run away like Jonah tried to do when God commissioned him to be a prophet. She could have run out to tell everyone how special she is: "The Lord is with me!" Instead, Mary stays with the angel, pondering this salutation. She searches for more profound meaning and significance for her life. She questions.

To *ponder* means to weigh, to consider, to mull over in the mind. Meditation and contemplation are disciplines of pondering. Both contemplation and meditation are about giving extended thought to or focusing on something. They are about seeing connections that may not be obvious at first. They allow us to move beyond the meaning of words to feel their emotional impact. They evoke responses within us like praise and thanksgiving and emotions like comfort and joy and fear and awe.

While Mary is meditating on this greeting of the angel, Gabriel continues his announcement. He explains that God plans to interrupt her life in a big way. She will conceive and give birth to a son who will restore the kingdom of his ancestor David. This kingdom will never end, and this child will be the Son of God. The child's description is reminiscent of God's covenant with David in 2 Samuel 7:8-16. There God speaks of David's kingdom as an everlasting kingdom and David's heir as God's Son. People have prayed for this for years. Mary likely prayed for this as a faithful Jew. But it's shocking—perplexing—to learn God is working out God's promises in us. We need time to consider, to weigh, to ponder God's message taking shape in us.

Mary continues to ponder, asking Gabriel questions, trying to understand how this is going to happen. She tries to penetrate the full meaning of these words. How can she, an unwed woman, who has not known a man, give birth to a son, much less the Son of God?

In response to this question, the angel points Mary back to another miraculous conception. Her cousin Elizabeth is now pregnant. Though Mary is young and not yet wed, Elizabeth is advanced in years and still childless. Now in her old age, Elizabeth is six months pregnant. Elizabeth's story reminds us of Old Testament stories of women who conceive after long infertility periods, women like Sarah, Rachel, and Hannah. However, Mary's story is new. She has not been married and hoping for children for years. She is engaged but not yet wed. God is doing something through this young woman that is different, "for nothing will be impossible with God" (Luke 1:37).

Luke never says Mary fully understood any of this, not the strange greeting or the miraculous promise. She ponders it, thinks deeply about the words spoken to her, and finally utters her acceptance, "Let it be with me according to your word" (Luke 1:38). Then the angel leaves her. Mary's acceptance of the pledge of God seems to be what the angel was after. Accepting the promise of God allows the words from God to come to life in her.

In Romans 1:3-4, Paul says the gospel is the message that Jesus descends from David and is the Son of God. Mary is the first to hear this message when Gabriel tells her she will give birth to this child. It is this gospel that she is meditating on. She receives the gospel and nurtures the Word of God within her through her pondering.

Then, like Gabriel, Mary leaves. Her contemplation moves her to action. Once we accept the word of God, it drives our lives. Luke says Mary moves with haste. Receiving God's message creates a desire to see what else God is up to in the world. Mary rushes to visit her cousin Elizabeth in Judea. I like to imagine Mary still pondering these words from Gabriel on her journey. She dwells on these words night and day as she makes her way to Elizabeth's house. In chapter 2, Luke will tell us again about Mary's meditation. After the shepherds visit the manger, Mary treasures and ponders what has happened in her heart (2:19). Later, when Mary and Joseph find the twelve-year-old Jesus in the Temple, we are told his mother treasured these things in her heart (2:51).

Elizabeth's greeting to Mary causes Mary to sing. Mary's *Magnificat* is her retelling of the gospel she has received. The song is the fruit of her pondering on the message of

Gabriel and Elizabeth's greeting. Like the psalmist, Mary finds comfort in meditating on God's promises: "This is my comfort in my distress, that your promise gives me life" (Ps. 119:50). The perplexing word has now become her comfort, and she shares this word in a joyful song.

Practice

- Read Psalms 44 and 107 and Isaiah 40 and 61. Then read the *Magnificat.* What echoes do you hear of these earlier passages in Mary's song? What other scriptural allusions can you identify in the *Magnificat*? Look at how phrases and words are used in earlier passages and then what new meaning emerges through the way Mary uses them in her song.

The Song of Rejoicing

When Elizabeth greets her, Mary breaks forth into singing. In some ways, Elizabeth's salutation is even more shocking than Gabriel's. Elizabeth says the baby in her womb leaped for joy at the sound of Mary's voice. She addresses Mary as the mother of her Lord. Mary's pondering allows her to hear this greeting as a confirmation of the promises Gabriel spoke to her. Meditating on God's word from the angel enables Mary to heed and welcome other signs of God's presence.

Whereas she was perplexed and pondered Gabriel's salutation, Mary now sings a song of praise that echoes the psalms of Israel. Three times in her greeting, Elizabeth calls Mary blessed. Mary's song, in response, is a statement of faith that this blessing is from God.

The *Magnificat*'s words resemble Hannah's song in 1 Samuel 2:1-10, sung after the birth of Samuel. Many of the phrases are similar, especially in the Greek translation of the Old Testament. The terms and phrases Mary sings are scattered throughout the Old Testament. Yet she weaves these old notes of praise into a new song of joy in response to God's working in her life.

Mary's praise magnifies God's work. The focus is not on her but on what God is working through her to fulfill God's promises. She celebrates God's work in bringing this blessing about and talks about it as an accomplished act. The verbs describing God's actions are in the past tense. However, like Advent itself, Mary's song combines past, present, and future. God has acted. Future generations will call her blessed because of God's action. In the middle is Mary, rejoicing. The Lord has done great things for her and deserves great praise. Between the promise and the fulfillment, there is the singing. Between the conception and the completion, we draw strength by focusing on God's past action, longing for God's future activity, and learning to see God's present work among us.

I used to hear the opening words of Mary's song, "My soul magnifies the Lord," and wonder, *How is that possible? How can we make God bigger? How can any human magnify God?* My discovery of the magnifying glass through my childhood collections helped me understand Mary's words differently. Mary is not making God bigger. Instead, she is raising our awareness of God's presence through her joyous song. Like a magnifying glass bringing hidden characters to light, Mary's song interrupts the narrative flow of these stories of miraculous birth, inviting us to think profoundly about what this means. Her song is like taking a deep breath to soak it all in. It invites us to stop and ponder what is happening. The *Magnificat* says there is more going on here than meets the eye. This act of God reaches back to previous visitations and promises, as well as looks forward to the fullness of God's kingdom and presence with us. Stop and consider, contemplate these words, and take in their full import. Raise your awareness of God, and you might find yourself breaking forth in joyful song.

Mary's song uses repetition to invite us to meditate on these words.[1] Hebrew poetry is built mainly on parallelism. Rather than rhyming words used to create a certain cadence, parallelism places two ideas next to each other, allowing them to enhance and interpret each other. The *Magnificat* has several examples of this poetic device. Verses 46 and 47 have two lines that express the same idea through different words, "My soul magnifies the Lord, and my spirit rejoices in God my Savior" (Luke 1:46-47). Magnifying God and rejoicing in God are synonymous expressions of Mary's focus on God. In verse 51, the second line expands and explains the first, "He has shown strength with his arm; he has scattered the proud in the thoughts of their hearts" (Luke 1:51). Scattering the proud is how God's strength is displayed. This expansion of thought, one idea carrying further an earlier image, is known as synthetic parallelism. Verse 52 uses antithetical parallelism to contrast what God does for the high and low in society: "He has brought down the powerful from their thrones, and lifted up the lowly" (Luke 1:52).

Parallelism invites us to slow down and expand our perception of God's action. Synonymous parallelism uses one idea to explain another, causing us to hold the two concepts together, letting them interpret each other. Rejoicing in God causes us to reconsider what it means to magnify God. Synthetic parallelism broadens our thinking using one thought to build on an earlier one. When has God scattered the proud and how? What other ways does God display strength? Antithetical parallelism invites us to contemplate through contrasting ideas. Does raising someone up demand lowering someone else? Or do the two concepts together envision a leveling of society?

Practice

- Mary's visitation of Elizabeth is another popular theme in artwork. Search different paintings to see how Mary and Elizabeth greet each other.
- The *Magnificat* is often compared to Hannah's song in 1 Samuel 2:1-10. What similarities and differences do you notice between the two songs?

Celebrating God's Salvation

M ary focuses our attention on the works of God. Her singing is like a reversal of the garden of Eden. In Eden, trouble occurs when Adam and Eve try to put themselves in place of God. In the Garden, we lost sight of God and emphasized ourselves. Mary draws our attention to God in explosive rejoicing over God's great reversals. She begins by magnifying God's work in her, and this leads her to see God's action in her in line with God's earlier and future works of salvation.

Magnifying and *rejoicing* share the same root in the Greek language. These activities are connected. Magnifying the work of God leads to joyfully celebrating God's actions. Mary's joy is in God, not gifts of God but God's faithfulness and mercy, attributes of God. Her rejoicing over God's saving work evokes memories of God's earlier works to save Israel. The tone of Mary's song reminds us of Miriam singing after the crossing of the Red Sea in Exodus 15 or Deborah celebrating the victory over Israel's enemies in Judges 5. In response to God's salvation, Miriam and Deborah break into ecstatic song. Mary sings joyously of God's work in and through her. She sings of God's certain victory through God's promise growing within her.

Focusing on God cultivates humility in Mary. Seeing God for who God is allows us to see ourselves as dependent on God's mercy. Isaiah is prepared to be God's messenger only after his vision of who God is and how God can cleanse him (see Isaiah 6). Mary realizes that all that is happening to her depends on God's mercy; God looks on her lowliness with favor.

Mary gives thanks for what God has done for her. Yet she does not claim any entitlement to this. She celebrates God's choosing her as an act of God's grace. Gabriel never tells us why Mary found favor with God any more than the writer of Genesis explains why God chose Abraham and not somebody else to be the bearer of God's promises. Though God's grace is personal, calling Abraham and singling out Mary, it is not individualistic. God called Abraham to be a blessing to the nations. Like God did through her ancestor Abraham, God is working out through Mary something that is for all people. So her song progresses from a personal to a social scope.

In the first stanza of her song, verses 47-50, Mary recounts God's visit to her as a great reversal of fortune. The second stanza, verses 51-55, celebrates this reversal as a sign of God's reversal of society. What God has done in Mary, God will do throughout the social order. Again, Mary sings of these reversals as accomplished acts of God. *Mercy* is used in verse 50 at the end of the first stanza and repeated in verse 54 at the end of the second stanza. Mary frames God's coming—past, present, and future—as mercy reversing our fortunes.

Mary begins describing God's social reversals as worked out by the strength of God's arm. References to "God's arm" fill the books of Deuteronomy, Psalms, and Isaiah (for example, Deuteronomy 4:34; Psalm 98:1; Isaiah 63:12). This metaphor occurs in connection with God's destruction of the Pharaoh's army and making the Israelites victorious over the native inhabitants of Canaan. From the Passover in Egypt, Israel has seen God's intervention in history as a display of the strength of God's hand (see Exodus 13:3).

Mary's song of reversal points forward to Jesus' sermon in Luke 6, where blessings and woes balance each other. To speak of raising someone suggests the lowering of another. Jesus' sermon in Luke 6 is often referred to as the Sermon on the Plain. This title is metaphorical as well as literal. Jesus preaches from a level place about a leveling of society. Jesus does not envision a constant back and forth, where now the lowly are raised only to be lowered later. He speaks of an equal society. Long before Jesus' sermon, Mary sings about this new society as an accomplished act.

Mary's singing about these acts of God as already accomplished is an act of faith. Her faith grows from God's previous faithfulness to Israel's ancestors. She draws confidence and strength from God's keeping God's promises to Israel, as Elizabeth's pregnancy is meant to be a sign confirming for her what God will do through Mary. God will not lose sight of Mary any more than God forgot his promise to Abraham. God will accomplish what he spoke to her through the angel, as surely as Elizabeth is about to give birth.

While Mary sings about toppled kingdoms and lowering the proud, the *Magnificat* has the joy of birth to it. There are these two unexpected births of John the Baptist and Jesus, but more importantly, there is to be a birth of a new social order through their ministry.

Practice

- There are several musical settings for the *Magnificat*. You can find many recordings on the Internet or You-Tube. Listen to a few different arrangements. Which is your favorite? Why? How do different arrangements draw your attention to different parts of Mary's song?
- Read Exodus 15:1-21 and Judges 5. What similar moods or phrases do you see expressed in these hymns and the *Magnificat*?

The Spirituality of Magnifying

So what does it mean for us to continue to sing Mary's song today?

The *Magnificat* is often used at evening prayer in the Western church. It is a fitting way to celebrate the victories that God has brought about in our day. Many of these victories go unnoticed, and we fail to pause and give thanks for them. Taking up Mary's song causes us to ponder the things God may be doing in our lives and the world today, to marvel at what God does through us. Doubtless, many of God's workings through us will be unknown to us. We cannot always know what joy or comfort we might bring into someone's life. We may never see the relief our giving brings to others. We might be unaware of how God's presence in us has caused joy like Elizabeth experienced at the sound of Mary's greeting. In keeping with Mary's humility, it is probably best that we do not know more of these moments, less we forget to sing about the wonders of what

God is doing and start to think we are to be thanked or praised for such actions.

Placing Mary's song on our lips reminds us that we are to carry God's message into the world also. Hopefully, God's promises come to life within us in a way that brings God's presence to others. We have the responsibility of nurturing God's word within us like an expectant mother's body nourishes new life within. Perhaps this is why the Eastern church has traditionally used Mary's song at morning prayer, to welcome the new day with the possibility of carrying God's word into our world.

When Mary sings, Caesar is still emperor, and Herod is the king over her land. God's leveling is not complete. Mary starts singing amidst the birth pangs of God's kingdom. When we join Mary's singing, we join God's work in the world. We do not lose heart, nor do we sit passively waiting, because God's kingdom is not complete. Singing Mary's song stirs up our faith, causing us to tap our feet to God's rhythm. We hasten to spread the news of God's coming.

One way we can help God's word grow within us is to ponder God's promises to us like Mary pondered the angel's greeting. An excellent place to start is with the song of Mary. Meditate on these words. Read them again and again. Question the meaning of each term like Mary questioned Gabriel. Contemplate what the words could mean in your life. What would it mean to take these words of Mary to heart? Marvel at the possibilities. Question, the way Mary questioned the angel, "How can this be?"

Do we want to celebrate the kind of leveling of society that Mary joyously sings about? Mary's song is frequently sung in some of the most ornate churches of Christendom with robed choirs and expensive pipe organs providing accompaniment. In many ways, that may seem like the very antithesis of what Mary sings. That the words of this peasant, unwed, expectant mother now provide some of the most moving music in some of the world's most lavish settings is something Mary could not have imagined. Nor could she have guessed the countless artists who have tried to depict her singing her song or questioning the angel. But that we meditate on the scene and still find the words so moving may be part of the hope that caused Mary to celebrate God's reversal as an accomplished fact. The song will not let us go, as if we sense something is still not quite right in the world.

Pondering these words and these scenes interrupts our lives, causing us to magnify the presence of God in our settings. The life and ministry of her Son keep us from over spiritualizing Mary's song. Jesus preaches and practices concrete acts of exalting the lowly and lowering the proud. The songs of Advent and Christmas set us to the rhythms of God's redemption in the world. Charles Wesley's hymn "Come, Thou Long-Expected Jesus" celebrates Jesus as our comfort and joy. According to Wesley's text, Jesus' comfort releases us from the fears and sins that keep us from participating in God's work in the world, freeing us to participate in God's redemption joyfully. Like Mary, we ponder the mystery of God at work in and through us. Then we go forth singing, participating in God's salvation.

Practice

- Mary's song has inspired many hymns, including "My Soul Gives Glory to My God." Try singing the *Magnificat* through this or some other arrangement. What is different about singing the text versus reciting the words? How are you aware of different parts of the text when singing?
- How does Mary's song move you to join God's action in the world?

SECTION TWO
Zechariah's Song

The *Benedictus*: Luke 1:67-79

Context: Luke 1:5-25, 57-66

Blessing the God of Israel

"Blessed be the Lord God of Israel."
—LUKE 1:68

Joy is not something we usually associate with John the Baptist. We get so enamored with the image of the wild-eyed, bug-eating, desert prophet of repentance that we think joy is out of place in John's presence. Yet Zechariah, John's father, practically dances at the birth of John. At least, we know he sang after John's birth. His joy just had to come out.

I wanted to sing when my son, Matthew, was born. I did not. The doctors and nurses are probably thankful for that. I had all this emotion and excitement inside me, and it was challenging to keep it in. Later, when Kristen, Matthew, and I were in our hospital room alone, I took Matthew in my arms and sang softly to him while swaying to the tune's rhythm, releasing some of my joy. I made up the song as I was singing it. I no longer remember the words. I remember I used an old hymn tune; it was so ingrained in my memory that it was the easiest tune to draw on at the time. However, I was improvising the lyrics, using words to explain the meaning of Matthew's name and expressing how excited I was to meet him.

While growing up, singing was common in my household. My mother loved teaching her children hymns. My father had fun creating rhymes that he would sing for us. If we were not singing, there was usually a radio or record player on somewhere in the house. Now, music is part of the home that Kristen and I have made with Matthew. We enjoy a variety of musical styles. We sometimes make up lyrics of our own to songs we sing, occasionally because we do not know the correct words, but sometimes just to play around with the song. We have fun improvising with texts and tunes.

Matthew's interest in music took on a life of its own a few years ago. He started playing the guitar and began private lessons. He and some friends formed a band and would spend lunch most days during their eighth-grade year playing music. When he started high school, Matthew added a class in classical guitar and what would become his real passion, jazz band.

Matthew plays lots of musical styles and enjoys doing some composing, but he loves playing jazz. He loves to explain to me how jazz builds upon and alters established musical patterns. For him, the joy of jazz is knowing the fundamentals and tradition of music but being able to spontaneously create while playing, expressing the moment's emotion through improvised performance. "Dad, jazz is great because of the improvisation," he explains. That's the main thing he's been able to teach me so far.

Zechariah's story and his song after John the Baptist's birth are the kind of jazz Matthew tries to explain to me. Zechariah takes up some of the classical themes and meter of Israel's poetry, but he blends them in a unique way and to a new beat. His improvisation builds on respect for the tradition while bringing a new emphasis that makes us listen for something more, wondering how this new creation will resolve itself. It's like he is saying, "This is not just the same tune. Keep listening."

Zechariah's jazz is similar to the improvisation Advent invites us to experience in our lives. Advent says, "Yes, God did come once in human flesh. Yes, God comes to us today in the Word and Spirit. But there is more; Do not be content with this. It's not resolved yet! Keep alert! Keep the faith! Keep moving!"

Zechariah's song is a father improvising at the birth of a son, a made-up song to release some of the wonder and joy that he feels in his bones in such a way that words alone cannot express. The emotion just has to come out. It's put to rhythm, and the rhythm helps to lock words into place. The rhythm emerges from a tension that builds in Zechariah's own life, is improvised in his song, and still longs for resolution.

Practice

- Read Luke 1:5-25, 57-66. The *Benedictus* is used in many traditions in morning prayer. Include reading this canticle as part of your morning prayer practice for the next week. How do the words of this text influence your approach to the day?

The Mute Priest

Jazz moves along to the rhythm of the backbeat. Back-beat takes a traditional meter like 4/4 time and empha-sizes the beats that are generally unaccented. Most music in Western culture stresses the first and third beats, the downbeats. In jazz and blues music, the emphasis is on the second and fourth beats, the backbeat.

Zechariah's song builds around the meter of Israel's faith in God being able to accomplish what we often think is impossible. However, his story and the song that fol-lows place a stronger emphasis on the future, yet-to-be-accomplished aspect of God's intervention. The *Benedictus* emphasizes God's fulfillment of the promise as a sign that God is not finished. Stay alert. Keep the beat.

Luke introduces Zechariah and his wife as a righteous couple. They are pious, observing all the commandments. Both are from priestly lineage. They have been married for a long time and are getting old, but they have no child. Perhaps this is why Luke begins the introduction by say-ing they were both righteous. At that time, many thought infertility was a sign of disfavor with God. Luke says that is not the case here. There is tension in the first few lines of their story. Traditional interpretation does not fit the context of this couple. There's a different beat here.

Perhaps this is a good place to pause and remind ourselves that Advent and Christmas can be difficult for many families. The stories of miraculous births can be challenging for those who have longed for children and cannot conceive, have lost children, or have miscarried. We need to be careful in hearing and telling these stories. Not all righteous couples have children. Some choose not to have children; others choose to adopt. The birth of children is not a matter of how hard you pray. Despite all of our medical knowledge, all births still carry an element of mystery and the miraculous. This is a good season to include in our prayers petitions for those who have lost children or still long for children.

The story of Elizabeth and Zechariah sounds familiar to those who know the rhythms of the Old Testament. We fall into the recognized beat of Abraham and Sarah, Jacob and Rachel, Elkanah and Hannah. Isaac was born to the aged Abraham and Sarah. After her sister had already birthed several sons to Jacob, Rachel finally gives birth to Joseph and later to Benjamin. Samuel is born to Hannah after being ridiculed by Elkanah's other wife, Peninnah. Parents long for children. God intervenes. A son is born. The family line continues. **One,** two, **three,** four; the beat goes on.

But there is a twist in the promise of God's intervention here. The purpose of this child to be born to Zechariah and Elizabeth is not just to continue the family tree. John has a mission to prepare the way for one even greater, to herald the coming of the Lord. In his promise of John's birth, Gabriel already describes him as the Elijah-like prophet, pointing beyond himself to one greater. John's birth is in anticipation of God doing an even greater miracle. As joyous as this birth is, don't be content. There is more coming. One, **two.** There's a new beat emerging. This annunciation only builds our anticipation.

Practice

* Artists across the centuries have painted scenes of Zechariah being visited by Gabriel in the Temple and his singing at the naming of John. Explore some of these images on the Internet. A search of "Annunciation to Zechariah" and "Naming of John the Baptist" will lead you to icons and paintings of these events. What are some of your favorite depictions? Why? How do they capture Zechariah's astonishment in the Temple and joy at the naming?

Observing Silence with Zechariah

When he receives this news of an expected birth, Zechariah is serving as a priest in the Temple in Jerusalem. He is inside the Temple alone when Gabriel comes to him and tells him that God is about to send Zechariah and Elizabeth the child for whom they have been praying. This good news is the comfort for which they longed.

Surely a priest would be well versed in the traditions and rhythms of the Old Testament. Zechariah must have known the stories of Isaac, Joseph, and Samuel. Yet Zechariah asks for a sign to be assured this will occur, for he and Elizabeth are getting old.

Zechariah's protest is different from Mary's response later on. Mary wonders about the mechanics of her pregnancy. How can it happen when she has not known a man? Zechariah feels trapped by the ravages of time. He and Elizabeth have not been able to have any children so far, and their advancing years suggest decreasing likelihood that they will be parents. Mary's response is the awe of God doing something entirely new. Zechariah's is the weariness of knowing while God can do this thing, it sometimes takes years for God's promises to be fulfilled.

Zechariah's response takes us back to one of Israel's most familiar notes, the unexpected birth of Isaac to Abraham and Sarah. God visits them when Abraham is ninety-nine and Sarah is ninety. They have been waiting for nearly twenty-five years for God to fulfill a promise for a son (a promise made in their seventies?!). When God comes to them and says, "This is it. I'm finally making good on that promise. I will be back next year, and Sarah will have a son!" Abraham and Sarah both laugh in response to that pronouncement. Abraham falls on his face laughing before God in Genesis 17. Sarah laughs behind God's back in Genesis 18. They both laugh, and God tells them to name their son Isaac, which means laughter.

Zechariah had to know that story. It's one of the first notes in the lyrics of ancient Israel. Zechariah's response is not so much to doubt that God could do this as to search for a sign of when God will do this. He knew from the old stories that God could provide a child to parents who sometimes waited a long time for a child. He wants to know what sign will point to *when* God will do this thing. One, **two,** three. The rhythm's not done yet; wait for it.

Isaac is the sign given to Abraham and Sarah. He is a sign that God will keep all his promises to Abraham, no matter how long it takes. He is the resolution to the rhythm. Zechariah himself will become the sign that God is going to do this thing through his unborn son. Gabriel says that Zechariah will be mute until the day that this son is named John.

Zechariah, the priest, one who should be leading Israel in worship and praise, exits the Temple unable to speak. One, **two,** three, **four.** We are not hearing the rhythm of the patriarchs' song we know so well. This is not Hannah's hymn rehashed. There is a new beat to this tune. It's not done yet. Keep listening.

We have to wait a while. Throughout Elizabeth's pregnancy, Zechariah is mute. It's literally a pregnant pause. Zechariah does not speak again until after John is born. When we do hear from him, he doesn't merely talk. He breaks forth into a song that fits the rhythm of this unexpected backbeat of anticipation, a song born out of the gestation of silence, weighing God's promises while awaiting God's fulfillment.

Practice

- Read 1 Kings 19:11-18. Where do you go to hear the silence? Keeping silence can be difficult in our world; however, silence can open us to hear God in new and exciting ways. Experiment with keeping a time of intentional silence. Set a timer for five or ten minutes. Perhaps envision this scene from First Kings, or choose a word or phrase to focus on during this time. What do you hear?

The Song of Blessing

Zechariah does not speak immediately after the birth of his son. The delivery is like another soft downbeat, moving the rhythm forward. It is only eight days later, at the moment of the child's naming, that Zechariah's tongue is set free. The moment presents a crisis, striking a discordant note.

Elizabeth says the child is to be named John. Tradition and social convention try to pressure the parents to name the child after his father or another family member. Bystanders ridicule Elizabeth, "There's no one in your family by that name. You mean he will be called Zechariah like his dad." The angel told Zechariah to name the child John. This is a moment of deciding whether to move forward in faith, following the angel's pronouncement, or give in to the routine and familiar. We hear the backbeat, an unexpected accent. There is a new tension building.

Most crises of faith are not dramatic calls to renounce our faith or curse God. They are the subtler pressures to conform to the norm: "Everybody else is doing it. This is how it's always done. Don't be different." We need the rhythmic beat of faith to keep us moving to God's will. Spiritual disciplines like prayer, scripture reading, worship, and singing sustain our faith in such crucial moments.

We do not often think of singing as a spiritual discipline. Yet according to scripture, singing sustains our faith in some of the most challenging moments. Paul and Silas sing in jail at Philippi. Residents of Judah compile many of the psalms of the Old Testament while they are captives in Babylon. The songs of faith keep us from the temptations to conform or lose hope, allowing us to walk in the way of God's promises.

Swinging to the meter of Israel's trust in God, Zechariah steps forward to support his wife, to follow the angel's words. Zechariah writes on a tablet, "His name is John." It is the next downbeat. He will not give in to the pressure of tradition but is moving to a new emphasis on the ancient rhythm. One, **two**, three. What happens next is the unexpected accent. The mute priest breaks forth into singing. **FOUR.**

A song not only sustains our faith in times of trial but expresses our elation when prose fails us. Sometimes words need tempo and meter to convey the emotional import. Like Mary, Zechariah composes a song of joy rooted in Israel's praise idiom. Gabriel said that this child would cause many to rejoice and bring joy and gladness to Elizabeth and Zechariah. Neighbors and relatives rejoice with Elizabeth at John's birth. Everyone who hears about these things ponders them. Then we get to listen to his jazz.

Zechariah's song is a mirror image of Mary's song. Mary's song has two stanzas. The first expresses her joy over God's intervention in her personal life. The second celebrates God's reversal in the social order. Zechariah's song also divides into two parts. He begins where Mary left off, with the social sphere (see Luke 1:67-75). He then moves to what God will do through the person of John the Baptist (see vv. 76-79). Even in this structure, we can see Zechariah experimenting with the joys of improvisation. Mary celebrated what God did in and through her personally. Zechariah does not focus on God's favor toward him or even in John, but how God will use John to prepare for one even greater. Zechariah uses improvisation to say, "Do not merely focus on what God has done or what God is doing and will do through this child. Instead, look for what God will do through the one this child points to; it's of cosmic proportions."

Mary's song recounts God's blessings to her and Israel. Zechariah begins by blessing God. One of the priest's primary functions is pronouncing God's blessing on the people in Numbers 6:22-27. Like that benediction, Zechariah's song begins with blessing and ends with peace.

Blessing means God's favor or power or strength is granted to us. So what does it mean for us to bless God? We cannot give God more strength or favor, can we? Nor does it make sense to say we are returning God's power to God. To bless God in the Old Testament meant to praise or thank God for God's acts in history. Usually, the phrase is a joyous doxology, a summary act of thanksgiving for God's visitations. The pattern of the book of Psalms illustrates such blessing. There are five sections to the book of Psalms. The first four divisions all end with a statement of praise similar to Zechariah's opening words (see Psalm 41:13; 72:18-19; 89:52; 106:48). These doxologies at the end of the first four books of Psalms are like summary statements. It is as if the doxologies say, "In light of all that has been recounted above, all the characteristics of God and the acts of God that you have heard, we bless God." The blessings of God lead us to proclaim God as a blessing God.

Practice

- The *Benedictus* has been put to many musical settings. Listen to different arrangements. Which style helps you meditate on the words? How do different interpretations draw your attention to other parts of the text? How is hearing the text different from reading it?

Praising God's Mercy

Zechariah places the blessing at the very beginning, "Blessed be the Lord God of Israel, and here is why" (Luke 1:68, AP). Zechariah's praise grows out of the worship practices and hymnody of ancient Israel. His blessing improvises the rhythm of the psalms and songs of the Old Testament. His jazz begins with joyful praise, and the backbeat helps us understand why.

We hear in this song all the familiar notes of Israel's story. There is hardly a word in this song of Zechariah that does not appear several times in the Psalms and other sections of the Old Testament. Yet they are woven together here in a unique act of praise. The *Benedictus* is the song of one deeply rooted in the idiom and meter of the scriptures, who improvises in this situation to create a new song of God's comforting visitation and our joyous response.

Zechariah himself continues to be the sign of the angel's pronouncement. His singing is itself proof of what God has done, is doing, and is yet to do. In response to his act of faith in naming the child John, Zechariah's tongue erupts in a song of praise. God's mercy frees us to "serve him without fear" (v. 74).

The *Benedictus* is Zechariah's retelling of what the angel spoke to him about John in the Temple, much as Mary's song is a reworking of the gospel Gabriel shares with her. But Zechariah is not content with merely repeating Gabriel's message. He expands and develops it; he improvises on Gabriel's theme. In the first stanza, he celebrates the deliverance God brought through David, the preaching of the prophets, and how God freed the Israelites so they could worship God in fulfillment of the promises God made to Abraham. The second stanza anticipates God's future faithfulness.

Zechariah's hymn celebrates the freedom that God offers us. He describes this freedom negatively as a release from the power of enemies. Positively, God's freedom is the possibility to worship God and live in holiness. John's job in preparing people for this restoration is to call them to forgiveness of sins. He is not the political or military savior who rallies troops to combat enemies. He calls us to confront ourselves and be ready for God's appearance. John prepares us to meet a Messiah who guides us in the ways of peace.

The priest struck mute in the Temple, the place where all of Israel's worship traditions, customs, and practices are safely guarded, now sings of a different way of serving God. It will not be as everything was in the past or even as we might imagine. But it will be in accord with God's past mercy and faithfulness.

One day, the one to whom John points will speak about the destruction of the Temple. In 70 CE, the Romans will destroy the Temple. Here the once mute Temple priest

already sings about a new way to worship God, worship
rooted in Israel's faith and traditions, but put to a new beat
like the improvisation of a new day for the whole earth.

Practice

- Read Genesis 15 and Psalms 103–106. What echoes of
  these passages do you hear in the story of Zechariah or
  his song?
- Read Acts 16:25-34 and Ephesians 5:11-20. How does
  singing help sustain your faith?

The Spirituality of Blessing

E arly on, the church inserted Zechariah's song in the morning prayer service of Lauds. Originally, Lauds was a sunrise service, a time to welcome the sun and begin each day by praising and thanking God. The association comes from the first half of the last sentence, "By the tender mercy of our God, the dawn from on high will break upon us" (Luke 1:78).

This imagery hints at a cosmic and universal work of God that is underway. The dawn touches all of creation, not just Israel. Yet dawn speaks of a beginning, not an ending. This universal way of light and peace is emerging but has not reached completion.

It might be hard to sing this song if we watch the morning news first. There are plenty of signs and images that portray the shadow of death and violence. Beginning the day singing Zechariah's song commits us to walk in this way of light and peace. Zechariah strengthens our resolve to this commitment in the first stanza by recalling to our minds all the times that God has brought salvation and redemption in the past. They were all surprising, unexpected interventions of God. We begin the day remembering God's past faithfulness so that we can be faithful to God in this day. The song sets our feet to the rhythms of our trust and hope.

The *Benedictus* is a song meant to help us begin the day rejoicing in the victories of God and looking for new victories in the coming day. It is a song of comfort, encouraging us that no matter how difficult the days before have been, with this new day, we have the hope of God's new intervention. It sends us forth in the joy of the Lord.

Singing the song each morning also reminds us that we have a calling like John's. We are to prepare the way of the Lord by pointing others to Christ. The Swiss theologian Karl Barth kept a copy of a section of the *Isenheim Altarpiece* painting above his desk. It contains an image of John the Baptist. In the picture, John stands with his arm outstretched, pointing to Christ. John's arm and finger are disproportional; they are more prominent than the rest of his features. Barth understood this to be the painter's way of indicating John's primary task as pointing to Jesus. Barth says we have a similar vocation to point to the Messiah.

The kind of improvisation Zechariah practices has provided us some great works of art in the church's history. They raise the biblical stories before us in ways that open us up to contemplate God's work in our lives today. This is why many painters depict scenes from the Bible in a contemporary idiom (compare Fra Angelico's painting of the Annunciation to Mary from 1438 with that of John Collier from the twenty-first century). They are not trying to portray historical accuracy but to help us think about what it would be like for God to come into our situation.

Musical works also help us ponder the meaning and implication of scripture anew. Works like Handel's *Messiah* can take the words directly out of scripture and, by playing around with them through melody and singing, make us linger over each word until it penetrates our mind and begins to be absorbed in our bones.

Other music can practice the kind of improvisation of words that Zechariah sings. One of the most famous lyrical improvisations we know is Isaac Watts's rewrite of Psalm 98. Many people feel they have not celebrated Christmas until they have sung this song, which is kind of amazing. The song never mentions Jesus or his birth. The song is "Joy to the World." While it never mentions Jesus by name or his birth, sung in the context of Christmas, we can't help but hear references to Jesus' birth. However, the song could just as easily be sung during Advent. It reminds us that while Christ's reign has begun, it is not yet complete, and it gives the kind of joy we need to sustain us in our waiting.

Singing is one way we point others to Jesus like John the Baptist does. Luke says those listening to Zechariah sing stopped and marveled. They told others about these things and pondered them. Like crowds gathering around a band of Christmas carolers, people stop, consider, perhaps join in the song.

Zechariah's song introduces us to some of the fundamental rhythms of our faith: trust in God's faithfulness, dependence on God's mercy, and a continued sense of awe and wonder that God can always do more than we think or imagine. Zechariah's jazz tune invites us to live out these rhythms in our day and context. We do not have to feel bound to the steps of Abraham and Sarah, Moses, Elijah, or even Elizabeth and Zechariah. We may have to improvise. But the key to good jazz improvisation is first understanding the traditions and ways that have gone before us. By studying the scriptures, meditating on them, and contemplating each word, the tradition seeps into our bones and becomes available to move us to new beats in our days. The song is not done. One, **two**, three, **four**!

Practice

- Read Psalms 96 and 98. Then read the lyrics of "Joy to the World." What similarities and differences do you see? What phrases from Watts make this song fitting for Advent? How would it feel to sing this song at other times of the year?
- Try singing the words of the *Benedictus* to a hymn like "Blessed Be the God of Israel." What different parts of the text do you notice when you sing? Try singing the song to a different tune. How does a particular tune accent certain parts of the song?

SECTION THREE

The Angels' Song

The *Gloria in Excelsis*: Luke 2:13-14

Context: Luke 2:1-12, 16-20

Play "Angels we have heard" on High

Glorifying God

❧

"Glory to God in the highest heaven."
—LUKE 2:14

When I started serving as a pastor, I had stringent liturgical guidelines, especially regarding the separation
of Advent and Christmas. Advent is about the coming of
God. Christmas is about the birth of Jesus. There are beautiful and often neglected songs for Advent like "Lo, How
a Rose E'er blooming" and "Come, Thou Long-Expected
Jesus." Christmas carols are for Christmas, the days from
Christmas Eve through Epiphany, January 6.

Somewhere along the way, I developed a new liturgical
season. It's a middle ground between Advent and Christmas. I don't think any liturgical calendar has incorporated
it, though I know several pastors who also adhere to it. The
season is popular because many pastors and worship leaders hear the refrain each Advent, "When can we start singing Christmas carols?" I call this season "Angeltide." The

rule for Angeltide is this: If one of the assigned texts for a given Sunday mentions an angel, we can sing any song featuring angels, even Christmas carols. There are several carols featuring angels. It opens up lots of singing possibilities.

In the beginning observances of this liturgical innovation, I was stricter. The angel song had to relate to the scripture story read in worship that day. So, if the scripture was about the angel speaking to Joseph, then the song had to reflect that scene. You could not sing about the angels and the shepherds just because Joseph has a midnight angel conversation in the scripture of the day. Lately, I have grown more lenient in the application of this rule. If the scripture reading has an angel in it and an angel appears in the song, I'm likely to use it in worship.

This more lenient interpretation of Angeltide is related to one of my favorite carols: "Angels We Have Heard on High." I enjoy singing this song. It's too good to confine to the twelve days of Christmas. I can't wait to sing it each year.

As a child, I loved holding the "or-or-or-or-or—ia" as long as possible. (I also may have thought we were singing about Oreos for the longest time. I believe this was when my mother started pointing out the words to me as we sang from the hymnal.) It was also fun, growing up in small congregations of the rolling hills of east Georgia, to hear people trill their *r*'s as they nearly ran out of breath approaching the end of these glorias.

Another thing that made this song so exciting as a kid was the clear divide created in many of these congregations. Among these farmers, shopkeepers, homemakers, and children, few of us ever studied Latin. However, there were sharp lines of demarcation between those who sang "ex-chell-sis" and "ex-SELL-seas."[1]

The angels' song is the shortest of all the canticles in Luke's birth narrative. Yet it may be the most widely used of all the canticles. The angelic chorus has been used or alluded to in many Advent and Christmas songs. While the other canticles appear mainly in daily prayer offices, the *Gloria* made its way into the church's weekly worship life for centuries through the Greater Doxology. The daily prayer offices were practiced mainly by monastics and clerics. Everyone who attended Sunday worship sang the Greater Doxology.

The song of the angels interrupts and interprets the story of the shepherds in Luke 2. The angels not only tell of a wondrous birth but give us the words we need to express our praise and thanks to God for the One who is born. They teach and give us the means to glorify God.

Practice

- Read Luke 2:1-20. Listen to a recording of "Angels We Have Heard on High" with a full choir. Turn the volume up. Just try not to join in on the "glorias."

" Birth announcement"
to the Shepherds

Angels song has
inspired chorus for
2000 years.

The Glorious Herald

C hapter 2 of Luke opens up with a decree from the Roman emperor Caesar Augustus. Augustus brought an end to the Roman civil wars. This end to internal unrest inaugurated what is known as the Roman Peace, *Pax Romana*. For the Romans, this did not mean a cessation of military expeditions, conflict, and conquering. It merely implied Romans were no longer warring with Romans, so they could unite in a common cause to conquer the world. To the rest of the world, this *Pax Romana* did not seem so peaceful.

A particular class of heralds, the *fetiales,* shared official Roman decrees. These heralds were like ambassadors in the ancient world. They spoke the words of the emperor throughout the empire. They proclaimed war and peace, as well as other events of imperial significance. Their voice was the voice of the emperor.

Luke says Augustus decrees that all the empire should be registered for taxation purposes. We do not know of such an empire-wide taxation policy from Augustus. There was a census when Quirinius became governor of Judea.

Luke may have this census in mind. Undoubtedly, he wants this census to sound like the kind of decree that would have displayed Rome's might and power. Perhaps a declaration shared by the imperial heralds.

The census also helps move Luke's story along. Joseph and Mary travel to Bethlehem because of this census, even though Mary is close to giving birth. Bethlehem is overcrowded because all these people living in villages and towns had to return to be registered at the place of their ancestors. From his palace in Rome, the emperor directs a pregnant peasant woman's movement in Judea, no matter her condition. That's the Peace of Rome.

Luke interrupts a story about Rome's might and power to move people around and keep them all counted with the story of a birth that seems insignificant in comparison. Then he interrupts the story of this birth with a visit to some nearby shepherds. Finally, he interrupts the shepherds in their routine duties with another visit from an angel. God's coming to us interrupts our lives and gives them new meaning, a new orientation, and a new song.

The angel's sudden appearance is hard to miss. When the angel appears, the glory of the Lord enfolds the shepherds and the angel. In the Bible, glory denotes God's presence. Being in God's presence, or being exposed to God's glory, changes us. In Exodus, after Moses spends forty days on Mount Sinai in God's presence, he descends with a face so bright he has to wear a veil (see Exodus 34:29-35). Isaiah is purified and able to begin his prophetic ministry after seeing a vision of God's glory (see Isaiah 6). When the glory of the Lord appears, things change.

Angels are messengers from God, God's ambassadors. This angel is a counterpart to the heralds that would have proclaimed a decree from Augustus. When he speaks to the shepherds, his message is like a divine proclamation: "Fear not! I am bringing you good news of great joy for all people. Today a savior has been born in the city of David, Christ, the Lord" (2:10-11, AP). A decree went out from God to all the world that the Savior is not in Rome but a tiny, over-crowded Judean village.

This decree of the angel counters the edict from Augustus. Augustus's proclamation brought upheaval and violence to the land of Judea. The angel appears and brings news of a new world order. A very different Savior is born, one who brings a very different kind of peace. This peace sets the heavens to singing joyfully about God's comforting presence on earth.

Practice

- Read Exodus 34:29-35 and Isaiah 6. How is God's glory portrayed? What difference does it make in the lives of Moses and Isaiah?
- Sing or listen to "Hark! The Herald Angels Sing."

Contrast of Roman peace + the angels peace

Echoing the Angels

F or all the singing that precedes this birth—Mary's song about what God will achieve through her child and Zechariah's song about how his child will prepare a way for this Messiah—Luke relates the birth of Jesus in one verse: verse 7. It seems anticlimactic. We expect him to add a song here, one of his best tunes yet. Instead, Luke quickly shifts our attention to the fields outside Bethlehem.

We are so used to the rhythm of this story of Jesus' birth that we do not notice the abrupt shift. Luke does not linger over the birth or compose a lullaby for the newborn Jesus. He simply states the facts. Mary gives birth. She wraps the baby up and places him in a manger because the town is crowded. Shift scene.

In a few short verses, Luke has introduced us to the most powerful man in the empire, Augustus, who had reached the status of a living god by this point in Roman mythology. The senate gave him the name Augustus on January 16, 27 BCE. *Augustus* means the majestic or illustrious one. This title hails Augustus as a savior for bringing an end to the

Roman civil wars and spreading the glories of Hellenistic civilization by expanding the empire. Along with this title, Augustus begins to claim that he is "son of the deified one." This epithet refers to his adoption by Julius Caesar, who was proclaimed a god after his assassination. Augustus rises to power thanks to his adoption by Caesar.

Next, Luke mentions the local representative of this son of the god, Governor Quirinius. Finally, Luke relates the birth of the baby, what Luke set up in the previous chapter. Instead of lingering here and inserting another song, Luke quickly directs our attention to some of the most familiar figures of first-century Judea: shepherds. We journey from the power and opulence of Rome to everyday, ordinary fields of shepherds.

Luke does not say if these are good shepherds or bad shepherds. We do not know if they are young shepherds or old shepherds. We only know that they were watching sheep, which is what we expect shepherds to do. Yet Luke spends more time on these shepherds than on Augustus and Quirinius. We know these shepherds because an angel of God appears to them. For Luke, the significant people are those who hear and respond to God. Part of the message of Advent is that God can come to any of us, anytime, anywhere. The ones who receive and respond to God's presence get caught up in this great biblical narrative.

As the angel gives his proclamation, the shepherds are surrounded by the glory of God. Once the angels leave, the shepherds decide to go to Bethlehem and see the child lying in a manger. On finding the newborn, the shepherds tell about their angelic visit. Then they return to their fields. They do not return as the same shepherds to their old routine. As Moses and Isaiah are changed through their exposure to God's glory, these shepherds are changed. They become herald shepherds.

The shepherds tell everyone what was shared with them and what they saw and return to their fields glorifying God. The shepherds have taken up the message and singing of the angels. Being in God's presence, the glory of God, causes them to break forth in praise of God, glorifying God. Their lives and singing echo the sound of angels.

Practice

- Artists have depicted images of the angels singing to the shepherds, the shepherds visiting the manger, and the shepherds returning to the fields. Do an Internet search for depictions of each of these scenes. Compare a couple of different paintings for each scene. What do you notice after examining the paintings? How do they cause you to see the text in a new way?

The Song of Glory

As the Lord's glory surrounds the shepherds and the angel, suddenly, a host of angels appear and break forth into singing. We often see this scene enacted with children in bathrobes with towels for head coverings like the characters in *A Charlie Brown Christmas*, so it is easy to sentimentalize this heavenly host as just a large number of angels filling the skies. Perhaps paintings have fixed in our mind a vision of angels neatly arranged in musical sections of baritones, altos, tenors, and sopranos with harps in hand to accompany their song. Luke seems to have something very different in mind when he mentions this heavenly host.

The word translated "host" in verse 13 is the Greek word *stratia*.[2] In classical Greek, this word means an army or group of soldiers. *Stratia* occurs twenty-eight times in the Greek version of the Old Testament. In each Old Testament reference, the term refers to either an earthly or heavenly army.

The vision of the prophet in Isaiah 6 includes singing in the heavenly court. Seraphs surround God's throne, calling, "Holy, holy, holy is the LORD of hosts" (v. 3). This canticle is known as the *Sanctus*. The *Sanctus* uses a different word for host than what is in Luke 2:13. The Hebrew word in Isaiah is often transliterated *Sabaoth*. *Sabaoth* is used nearly three hundred times in the Old Testament. It always appears in connection to the name of God, as in "the LORD, the God of hosts" (2 Sam. 5:10; Amos 4:13). At times it is used only in connection with Lord or God. This title depicts God as the leader of Israel's armies (see 1 Samuel 17:45) and as the leader of angelic forces or the heavenly court (see 1 Kings 22:19). Isaiah sees this heavenly court at worship in his call vision (see Isaiah 6). This heavenly host above the fields of Bethlehem is a divine army singing a marching tune. Imagine if John Philip Sousa wrote a Christmas carol. That's the *Gloria*.

The *Sanctus* uses parallelism to celebrate God's glory. In the first line, the angels sing that God is "Holy, holy, holy." Holiness speaks of the separateness of God, the unique nature of God. That the angels proclaim God thrice-holy means God is far more than we can think or imagine. This holiness is part of God's glory. In the next line, the angels mention this glory of God as filling the earth. Like the angels above the fields outside of Bethlehem, the angels Isaiah hears unite heaven and earth. The Lord God of hosts is proclaimed thrice-holy by the heavenly court, and this glory fills the earth.

The angelic host at Bethlehem builds a new verse to this song. The host begins where the seraphs in Isaiah ended, "Glory to God in the highest heaven." The glory that before is said to fill the earth now resides with God in the heavenly heights. Then the host turns to earth where God's glory manifests itself as peace with us.

Practice

- There are many musical settings of the *Gloria*. A You-Tube search of "Gloria in Excelsis" will lead you to these. Try listening to different arrangements. Which composition captures the mood and meaning of the *Gloria*? Which arrangements cause you to pay more attention to certain words in the *Gloria*? What arrangements do you think are distracting or inadequate for the *Gloria*?

Entering God's Peace

This army of angels singing glory to God outside of Bethlehem contrasts with the might of Rome. Augustus has his armies spread throughout the earth. Jesus has a host in the heavens. The legions of Rome imposed the *Pax Romana*. These angels sing of a very different kind of Savior with a very different kind of peace. There is also a war or battle theme running through the life and ministry of Jesus. Jesus goes into the desert to confront Satan after his baptism. His healings and miracles are battles with demons, Satan's minions. In Matthew's Gospel, when the crowd comes to arrest Jesus, and one of the disciples strikes out at the attackers, Jesus rebukes the disciple by saying, "Do you think that I cannot appeal to my Father, and he will at once send me more than twelve legions of angels?" (Matt. 26:53). Luke seems to have this cosmic battle in mind already at the birth of Jesus. Satan, like Augustus, has his armies. Jesus has this host of angels.

In the songs we have already heard, Mary and Zechariah's pieces, there are references to "savior" (1:47, 69). We hear this term and think of salvation from sins. In the Old Testament, the military leaders of Israel were often called "savior" (2 Kings 13:5, the word for *savior* here, *moshiah*, is often translated "deliverer," for example in Judges 3:9, 15). They saved people from destruction and death. This militaristic background to the word *savior* also builds the contrast with the image of Augustus as savior. The heavenly host sings in response to the proclamation of the first angel that the real savior has been born in Bethlehem. He will wage battle on the forces of sin and win, releasing us to praise God and live in God's peace.

Peace is another crucial concept in Old Testament theology. *Shalom*, the Hebrew word for peace, is more than not being at war or in dispute. Shalom is a sense of wholeness, of everything being suited to its purpose. Shalom involves all of creation living in harmony. Isaiah speaks of a peaceful kingdom where animals and humans live together without natural fears and hostilities (see Isaiah 11:1-9). Toward the end of the book of Isaiah, the hills sing and the trees clap at the approach of those living in God's peace (see Isaiah 55:12). Living in God's peace seems to call nature to join in the praise of God as well.

This proper worship of God means knowing who God is. Part of Isaiah's call is a new understanding of God. When Isaiah sees this vision of God and the heavenly worship, it causes him to confess his sin and the sin of his people, none of whom are able to praise God properly because of their unclean lips. Isaiah's confession prompts one of the seraphs to cleanse his lips with one of the coals. Now Isaiah can join in the praise of those surrounding God's throne.

Isaiah's book opens with a scathing critique of the Israelites who do not properly worship God: "The ox knows its master, the donkey its owner's manger, but Israel does not know, my people do not understand" (Isa. 1:3, NIV). The people worshiping idols and false gods are like animals who do not know where to find their food. On the other hand, the shepherds to whom the angels sang outside of Bethlehem will find their Lord in a manger (see Luke 2:11-12). How could they ignore the signs in light of this marching tune from the heavenly army of angels?

The angels never force the shepherds to go to Bethlehem. They tell the news modeling correct worship of this savior with their heavenly chorus. Then they leave. The shepherds now have a decision whether to journey to see if this news is true or stay put and dismiss this as a strange night in the fields. Unlike Augustus, who decrees that people have to move here and there and be counted, God does not coerce us into worship. God invites us and grants us the freedom of our response.

After finding their master in a manger just as the first angel said they would, the shepherds return glorifying and praising God, echoing back the tune they learned from the angels, "Glor-or-or-or-ia in excelsis Deo!" It's hard to hear that song and not join in. You don't have to wait until Christmas to sing it.

Practice

- The book of Isaiah has many references to peace. Read Isaiah 11 and 52:7-12. How is God's peace described in these passages?
- Many Advent and Christmas hymns refer to God's peace: "O Little Town of Bethlehem," "Silent Night," "It Came Upon a Midnight Clear," to name a few. Sing two or three of these songs. How do they depict God's peace?

The Spirituality of Glorifying

In the United Methodist Communion liturgy, we have a song that is a combination of the *Sanctus* and the *Gloria*. The minister introduces this song with these words, "And so, with your people on earth and all the company of heaven we praise your name and join their unending hymn:

> Holy, holy, holy, Lord, God of power and might,
> Heaven and earth are full of your glory.
> Hosanna in the highest.
> Blessed is he who comes in the name of the Lord.
> Hosanna in the highest." (UMH, no. 7)

The three holies recall the *Sanctus*. The *Sanctus* assigned God's glory to earth. The *Gloria* begins with God's glory in the highest heavens. The two songs together proclaim that the glory of God fills heaven and earth. The last three lines are taken from Jesus' triumphal entry into Jerusalem, "Blessed is the one who comes in the name of the Lord! Hosanna in the highest heaven!" (Matt. 21:9).

In Luke's Gospel, the words the disciples sing to welcome Jesus into Jerusalem on Palm Sunday are "Blessed
is the king who comes in the name of the Lord! Peace in
heaven, and glory in the highest heaven!" (19:38). In Luke
2, the heavenly host sings about peace on earth. In Luke
19, the disciples sing about peace in heaven and echo the
glory of the highest heavens about which the angels sang.
First, we hear a proclamation from heaven about peace on
earth. Then we hear the voices of earth praising the peace
of heaven.

Many scholars think that these two choruses were sung
antiphonally in the early church. One person or group sings
the song of the angels, and then a counterpart sings back
the song of the disciples from Palm Sunday. Out of this jux-
taposition and combining of some of these biblical canticles
grows the Greater Doxology.

Doxa is the Greek word used to translate the Hebrew
word *kavod*, meaning "glory." A doxology in the church
is a little song of praise, often drawn from scripture. By
the second and third centuries, it was popular to combine
some of these melodic scripture passages in imitation of the
biblical psalms, the sort of construction that went into the
songs of Mary and Zechariah. Learning how to praise God
was thought to be part of the purpose of worship. Songs
attributed to the angels in scripture took pride of place in
corporate worship. What better way to learn how to praise
God than to mimic the worship of heaven? By placing these
words of heavenly worship on our lips, we make worship
on earth as it is in heaven. So the *Sanctus, Gloria,* and canticles from John's visions in the book of Revelation became
some of the first hymns of the church.

The Greater Doxology was used in Latin and Greek for centuries in weekly worship. This doxology begins with the words of the *Gloria* and combines the *Sanctus* from Isaiah and other lines from biblical canticles. Generations of Christians had the rhythm and words of these angelic choruses embedded in their memories through this constant exposure.

As they did for the shepherds in the fields that first Christmas night, the words and tunes of these choruses not only get into our mind and heart but also move us to search for God's presence in our midst today. As we go, we find ourselves humming an angelic tune, holding out for the glor-or-or-or-ia of God. We march with a band of angels to the beat of God's glory and peace.

Practice

- Find a copy of the Greater Doxology. See if you can identify the various passages of scripture combined in this hymn of praise.

Shudy
Arden's preg   L.6   ♂
Clay

SECTION FOUR

Simeon's Song

The *Nunc Dimittis*: Luke 2:29-32

Context: Luke 2:22-28, 33-38

Departing in God's Peace

*"Master, now you are dismiss-
ing your servant in peace."*
—LUKE 2:29

I was serving as Sarah's pastor when I got the phone call. I knew Sarah mostly by phone. She moved to a retirement community about ninety miles away from our congregation years before I became the pastor there. I visited her a few times on her birthday but mostly encountered her through phone calls every six to eight weeks. This phone call was from Sarah's nephew. She was now under hospice care and not expected to live much longer. She asked if I could visit. By the time I got to her, she was awake and conscious but barely speaking.

I asked if Sarah remembered me. She nodded yes. I asked if I could pray for her. She nodded yes. I asked if there was anything about which I should pray. She did not respond. After a few moments of silence, I prayed for

God's comforting presence and the peace of the Holy Spirit to embrace Sarah. Those attending her said Sarah had not talked for a few hours. I mentioned the names of some of her friends in our congregation. Her eyes suggested that she recognized the names, but still, she said nothing.

I remembered Sarah once told me she loved the Psalms. In the silence, I started to recite Psalm 23. I was startled as halfway through the psalm Sarah started to say the words with me. After that, I began Psalm 100; she recited the words along with me. We said Psalm 121 in unison. I was afraid I would not remember any other psalms correctly, so I opened my Bible and read Psalm 8. Sarah recited it from memory. We read three or four other psalms together. I offered a prayer of thanks for our time together saying those psalms and left. Sarah died later that night. The message I received was that she never spoke again after I left the room. Everyone in that room was amazed at how comforted and contented Sarah seemed as she recited the words of those psalms. When words seemed to fail her, she could recall clearly the promises of scripture. Those words from scripture, etched in her mind, were not only the last words she spoke but also the source of peace during her final hours.

Simeon's song of peaceful departing is a mixture of pieces of the Psalms and songs of ancient Israel drawn together to express the comfort and joy he feels as he holds Jesus in his arms. He sees in this small child the Savior of the world. This perception bubbles forth in his song. Singing his song helps us rest in the assurance of God's promises as we embrace God's presence with us. The peace of God's presence releases us to go wherever God sends us.

Simeon's song is a perfect Advent hymn. It acknowledges that we live in the tension of God's past having come to us in Jesus, God's present activity currently working among us, and God's fullness of presence anticipated for the future. Whether this fullness appears in our lifetime or not, we can depart in the peace of God's presence already with us. Taking up God's presence with us as Simeon takes the baby Jesus in his arms, we are confident that God's salvation will reach its full purposes.

The few verses surrounding Simeon's canticle paint a portrait of a faithful disciple receiving God's peace. He is a model of what it means to receive Christ. Simeon first catches a glimpse of God's peace approaching in this family with a young child. Next, he holds the gift of peace, taking the baby Jesus into his arms while he sings. Finally, he says he is set free to go in God's peace. Singing the canticle helps us to see, celebrate, and peacefully accept God's coming to us.

Practice

- Read Luke 2:22-38. Roman Catholic, Lutheran, Anglican, and Orthodox churches include the *Nunc Dimittis* in prayer services at the close of the day. Recite the words before going to bed. How does this song help you rest in God's peace? What thoughts or images come to mind as you recite the canticle?

The Ecstatic Prophet

A man stands waiting in the Temple. Yet this is not the passive waiting of one idly passing time. Simeon is not a man with nothing better to do, letting time go by leisurely. This man represents the active waiting of Advent. He hopes to see the Lord's Messiah. He is expectant. He scans the crowd, searching from face to face, looking for some sign that God's promised comfort for Israel has come. Simeon is living off the promises of God—not only God's promises to Israel as a whole but also God's promise of a coming redeemer, salvation, and consolation. Simeon lives off the personal assurance from the Spirit that he will not die before seeing the Messiah.

I imagine Simeon rising early in the morning, shuffling to the Temple as soon as he can. I think many days he arrives before the gatekeeper's official opening time. He moves through the gate, finding a spot that gives the best vantage point to see the crowd coming and going. Simeon still has work to do. He longs to glimpse God's peace. He studies the scriptures to familiarize himself with all God's promises to Israel. He knows Malachi 3:1: "The Lord whom you seek will suddenly come to his temple." Simeon comes regularly and expectantly to the Temple, seeking the Lord's appearance. His meditation on the scriptures prepares him to recognize signs of God's coming.

Luke describes Simeon as a prophet. Three times in three verses (2:25-27), Luke mentions the Spirit in connection to Simeon. The Spirit rests on this man, reveals things to him, and guides him. Yet Simeon does not rest on these promises and promptings of the Spirit. He does not wait for God to come to him with the fulfillment of these words. Simeon actively responds to the Spirit. He wants to be ready for this revelation and not miss it. He goes out daily, looking for evidence that God is fulfilling these promises. He shows up to the Temple, hoping something extraordinary will occur within the ordinary daily activities.

Through the crowd in the Temple, Simeon notices a family approach. Luke describes the Holy Family as coming to fulfill the requirements of the law of Moses. There is nothing extraordinary in that. Most people in the Temple are there fulfilling requirements of the law. Simeon observes something more going on here.

Luke not only underscores Simeon's prophetic status through his repeated references to the Spirit working in Simeon's life but also highlights the prophetic gift of vision in connection to Simeon. Again, Luke refers three times to vision and Simeon. He introduces Simeon as one "looking forward to the consolation of Israel" in verse 25. Verse 26 says that the Holy Spirit revealed to Simeon that he would see the Messiah before seeing death.

While we often think more about the Old Testament prophets speaking, ecstatic visions were just as much a part of their ministry. Remember, Isaiah 6 records the call of the prophet through a vision of the Lord. Most of Ezekiel's preaching comes from visions the prophet receives. The book of Amos opens with the following: "The words of Amos, who was among the shepherds of Tekoa, which he saw concerning Israel" (1:1). It is common for the Old Testament prophets to "see" the word of the Lord before they speak. Simeon's song joins the chorus of prophetic visionaries.

Practice

- Artwork can help us see the stories of scripture. We have used art to meditate on the scenes of the earlier canticles. Look at some different artistic depictions of the scene of Simeon in the Temple. How does the art draw your attention to something that you did not notice in hearing or reading the text? How does the artwork inspire you to go back and read the text with new eyes?

Seeing Salvation with Simeon

Luke's description of the Holy Family's visit to the Temple hints at two ritual practices they observe. Like Simeon, Luke portrays them as devout members of Israel. The first practice is the sacrifice for Mary's purification. Leviticus 12 describes the rite of purification for a woman after childbirth. Forty days after a male child's birth, the mother is expected to sacrifice a lamb and a pigeon or turtledove. If the family is poor, the sacrifice can be two turtledoves or pigeons. The family Simeon focuses on brings two birds for their sacrifice. Simeon sees a peasant family come to offer their sacrifice. There could be little remarkable about that. Undoubtedly, the majority of the people coming and going to the Temple are poor.

The other ritual Luke alludes to in connection with this Temple visit is the practice of presenting the firstborn male child to the Lord. This rite goes back to the Passover in Egypt, described in Exodus 13. God passes over the Israelites' homes, sparing their firstborn male children on the night when the firstborns of the Egyptians are struck down. The Israelite firstborn males are then to be consecrated to the Lord. Later, when the tribe of Levi is set aside to serve the Lord, the firstborn of other tribes is allowed to be redeemed or bought back from the Lord through an offering of five shekels (see Numbers 18:16). Luke does not mention the offering for the redemption of Jesus. Instead, the story is interrupted by the aged Simeon taking the baby in his arms and singing about the fulfillment of God's promises through this child who will redeem us.

Simeon sees more than a poor family fulfilling their ritual duties. He sees the hope of Israel in the presentation of this child. Simeon sees more than the physical events transpiring. He perceives world-changing significance in this gift. He sees God's salvation for the world offered in this child.

Like the visions of the prophets, Simeon's seeing is about more than what meets the physical eye. This seeing detects the work of God in the events unfolding. He sees a poor family come into the Temple to offer their sacrifices for purification and dedication, but he perceives that in this child, the consolation he has been longing for approaches. It is this consolation that the Spirit promised he would see. The Spirit told Simeon he would not see death before seeing the Messiah. So he goes to the Temple, expecting to behold this consolation of Israel.

Consolation is another word for comfort. Comforting someone in sorrow is our most common use of the word *consolation*. Isaiah refers to God's coming to restore Israel as God comforting Israel (see Isaiah 12:1; 40:1-2; 51:3; 52:9). The passages in Isaiah 51 and 53 speak of God's

restoration of Israel causing the people to respond with joyful singing.

Simeon's perception that Israel's consolation approaches
in this child is rooted in his meditation on the promises of
God to Israel. His song is a patchwork of Old Testament references, particularly the vocabulary of Isaiah 40–55. What
he sees and sings about in this child he holds is the fulfillment of God's promises. His meditation on God's promises
allows him to see God's presence, causing him to break
forth into joyful singing.

Practice

- Read Genesis 46:28-30; 1 Samuel 3; Isaiah 42, 44, and
  52. What role does vision or seeing play in these texts?
  What connections do you see to the story of Simeon?

The Song of Consolation

S imeon takes the child into his arms and begins his song. His little ditty is the climax of the birth narrative canticles. The earlier canticles have been leading up to this proclamation. He picks up previous themes of peace, salvation, and light but adds to it the Gentiles. What God is accomplishing through this child is not just personal salvation or salvation for Israel. Simeon clarifies that the angels sang about Jesus as God's gift of peace on earth, including the Gentiles—the other nations—alongside Israel. Simeon sings about the universal nature of salvation.

Simeon's opening words take us back to Mary's song. In celebrating God's great reversal of lifting the lowly and bringing down the proud, Mary identified as the servant of God. Simeon, similarly, identifies as God's servant. The Old Testament commonly uses the term *servant* to speak about Israel's role in God's redemption. There is a series of Servant Songs in the latter half of Isaiah (chapters 42, 49, 50, and 52–53 together form four songs). Christians interpret these songs as references to the life and ministry of Jesus.

Jews understand them as references to Israel as God's servant in the world. Before the first Servant Song there is another reference to Israel as God's servant in Isaiah 41:8-10 (CEB):

> You, Israel my servant,
>> Jacob, whom I have chosen,
>> offspring of Abraham, whom I love,
>> you whom I took from the ends of the earth
>>> and called from its farthest corners,
>> saying to you, "You are my servant;
>> I chose you and didn't reject you":
>> Don't fear, because I am with you;
>> don't be afraid, for I am your God.
>> I will strengthen you,
>> I will surely help you;
>> I will hold you
>> with my righteous strong hand.

Here Israel is identified as God's servant since God's call of Abraham. Israel should take courage in God's presence among them. By identifying as God's servant, Simeon represents faithful Israel longing for God's visitation. His song bursts forth from the renewed vigor of holding God's presence in his arms.

Simeon's service is like that of a watchman, vigilantly looking for signs fulfilling God's promises. The Old Testament uses the metaphor of a watchman to describe the ministry of the prophets. Like those who would mount the city's walls, scanning the horizon for signs of danger, the prophets looked for warning signs to share with Israel regarding God's activity in the world. Simeon's watch is now over. The promise that he would see the Messiah before his death has been kept. Now he descends his watch post in peace.

The idea of peaceful rest as a reward for faithfulness stretches back through the Old Testament promises. In Genesis 15:15, when God forms a covenant with Abraham, God promises Abraham that he shall die in peace at an old age. Toward the end of Genesis, when Jacob sees his son Joseph, whom he thought was dead, Jacob says, "Now I can die, because I have seen your face" (46:30, AP). Isaiah 57 promises that the righteous will be granted peace and rest (see vv. 1-2). The opening line of Simeon's song echoes these biblical promises of peace for God's faithful sentinels, "Master, now you are dismissing your servant in peace, according to your word" (Luke 2:29).

Holding Jesus in his arms, Simeon feels Israel's consolation, the long-awaited fulfillment of God's promises through the ages. Simeon sings about more than personal comfort. He sees this child taking God's salvation to all the nations. His song is a lullaby about the hope of the world offered through this child.

Practice

- Find a few different musical arrangements of the *Nunc Dimittis*. See if you can find versions from different cultures and nations, remembering that it is a song about universal salvation. Which arrangement helps you hear the text better than others? How does a particular arrangement bring out certain aspects of Simeon's song that you had not noticed before?

Extending God's Salvation

S imeon did not make up this song of universal salvation
out of the air. It is deeply rooted in the stories of God's
purpose for Israel. In the call of Abram, we hear that all
the families of the earth will be blessed through the patri-
arch (see Genesis 12:1-3). Israel was to be light to the other
nations, showing them how to walk in the ways of God.
This idea of the ministry to the other nations is prominent
in the latter part of Isaiah.

Both Isaiah 49:6 and Isaiah 52:10 speak of all the nations
seeing the salvation of God. Psalm 25:5; 40:1; 119:166, 174
are all verses that talk about waiting for God's salvation.
Isaiah 25:9 tells how joy emerges from finally seeing the
Lord after years of waiting. In Luke 2:30, Simeon picks up
these notes of longing for salvation and the joy of fulfillment
through the simple line, "My eyes have seen your salvation." It is this vision that allows him to depart peacefully.

The final two verses of Simeon's song are the kind of
synonymous parallelism that we see in Mary's song. Simeon
states the same idea in different words but in a way that

expands the meaning of what we first hear. He begins by saying that this salvation has been prepared before all people. The angels sing about peace on earth for all. The last lines bring this home in a new and powerful way. Simeon mentions one of the most visible lines of demarcation for many faithful Jews living in this land occupied by the foreign Roman armies: Jew and Gentile. This child is to be the Savior bridging this gap.

All the Servant Songs in Isaiah talk about the light of God's salvation attracting the Gentiles to the mountain of God. Simeon is standing in the Temple built atop that mountain, singing that this child is the fulfillment of that ancient pledge. But this light to the Gentiles is not a rejection of Israel; it is the glory of Israel. This light to the nations is the fulfillment of a promise that reaches back to the call of Abraham in Genesis 12:3 that all the nations of the world will be blessed through Abraham. Simeon perceives this child to be God's making good on that promise.

Psalms 96, 97, and 98 speak of joy and ecstatic songs that break forth at the sighting of God's salvation. According to Psalm 97:6-8, the revelation of God's righteousness will lead the nations to renounce their false worship and worship the true God, which will bring glory to Zion and rejoicing to Judah. All three of the psalms connect revelation to all the earth of God's salvation with glory and joy. These are all themes we see woven together in Simeon's song.

Holding God's peace frees Simeon to sing his song of praise. He can descend his watchman's post as a faithful servant. God's work is not complete yet, but Simeon holds the living sign that this work is begun. The child he holds is also a reminder that this salvation is not dependent on

Simeon. He is not responsible for bringing it to completion, but Simeon can take consolation in its presence. His job is to let people know that the peace and salvation we long for, the peace that will reconcile Israel and the Gentiles, humans and God, is present in this child. So he lifts his voice in a song like a town crier calling out in the night, "Rest in peace, God has sent a light that is just dawning and cannot be extinguished."

Practice

- Read Genesis 12:1-9; 15:1-16 and Psalms 96 and 97. In what ways do you see Jesus fulfilling the promises and hopes shared in these passages?

The Spirituality of
Letting Go

S ince the fourth century CE, Simeon's canticle has been a part of night prayer services in the Eastern Orthodox and Western Catholic churches. The Orthodox churches of the East place the canticle in their vesper service. In the Roman Catholic churches of the West, the canticle is sung at compline, the night prayer service. Protestant churches that retain daily fixed-hour prayer liturgies continue the tradition of using the *Nunc Dimittis* during the nighttime prayers.

The words of the canticle invite a peaceful night's rest. The song reminds us that such peaceful repose is a gift of God. Singing the song before going to bed for the night is a confession of faith. We trust that God will be faithful to the promises of peace to us, as God was faithful to Simeon long ago. We can rest in God's peace.

Trusting the faithfulness of God's promises is part of the Advent message. We remember God's coming through Jesus in keeping with the promises to David, Abraham, and all the generations of expectant Israelites. We open ourselves to God's presence among us today in Word and Spirit. Yet we know God is not done; the promises are not completely fulfilled. We long for the coming of God to be fully present with us. Until that day, we rest peacefully, trusting God's faithfulness.

Like Simeon, our resting is not passive watching from the sidelines. We look for signs of God's coming to us and prepare to celebrate those signs. We also are prepared to join in God's work of salvation. God's work means not only a personal working out of salvation, growing in our relationship with God, but also participating in God's acts in society, the kind of works of justice and mercy that Mary's song puts into our hearts and mind.

In the Lutheran tradition, the *Nunc Dimittis* is sung after receiving Communion. Having eaten the bread and drunk the wine, we have held and consumed God's promised presence with us. Feeding on this life of Christ strengthens us to go forth and join in God's work in the world. It is not that we go forth to work out God's salvation in our strength and power but through God's grace at work within us. God's presence sets us free to carry forth God's work in the world,

Simeon reminds us that our work is never complete. He sings of a salvation that unites the nations. We know that even now, this work is not complete. But still, we can rest in God's presence. We can draw strength from trusting that God will keep the promises of God's coming to us. The salvation Simeon longs for is beginning, but these are only the green sprouts of spring. The culmination is a long way off.

John Wesley believed that we are all called to be perfected in love. He thought we are called to strive for this in our present life. He also cautioned that he believed few of us ever attain such perfection, and he never claimed it for himself. He saw perfection in love as a goal, causing us to continually work with God, continuing to grow in love of God and one another. Singing Simeon's song encourages us to keep participating in God's works of salvation—but not so frantically as if we think it all depends on us. We can repose in God's peace while joyfully joining God's service. "Lord, now You are letting Your servant depart in peace, According to Your word" (Luke 2:29, NKJV).

Simeon joins the long chorus of biblical characters who sing of God's faithfulness to God's promises: the psalmists, Deborah, Moses, Miriam. Themes of seeing salvation, sight for all peoples, a light to the Gentiles, and glory to Israel, which appear in the *Nunc Dimittis,* dominate the latter half of Isaiah. Yet these are ancient rhythms of Israel, tapped out centuries before when Miriam took up her tambourine at the shores of the Red Sea and when David danced into Jerusalem. Singing Simeon's song tunes our hearts to signs of God's faithfulness among us today.

Taking up the child Jesus in his arms frees Simeon to praise God. Holding God's peace sets us free from our fears and compulsions. God's peace is freedom *for* as much as freedom *from.* It is freedom for true praise to God and freedom from our sins. It is freedom for loving one another and freedom from our hostility toward others. God's peace also frees us to join God's work in the world.

Simeon saw in a poor family entering the Temple with a new child the fulfillment of God's promises to him, which was about God's promises to Israel, which was about God's promises for all: a light to the nations. How can we not join in that singing?

Perhaps we feel like we cannot sing Simeon's song because we are not sure salvific things are happening in the world today. That may be the very reason to sing this song. As Simeon studied and meditated on God's promises of scripture to discern signs of God's fulfillment in his day, his song sets our lives to the rhythm of God's promises, reminding us what we should be looking for in our day. When we do see such signs of God's presence among us, how can we keep from singing? Often it is a song that bubbles up from the deep resources of our faith, tuning our lives to the rhythms of God's promises.

Most of the people gathered in the Temple that day saw a poor girl with her baby led by her working-class husband. Through faith, Simeon saw the redemption of God at work. So let us take this Christ into our arms and trust that because of Christ in us, we too can rest in God's peace. Reconciliation among the nations is still unfinished work and still difficult, but holding Christ, we realize it does not rest on us, and we do not lose hope because we see God's work already set loose in us.

Practice

- Charles Wesley's hymn "Come, Thou Long-Expected Jesus" has strong echoes of the song of Simeon, particularly in the first verse. How does singing this song help you meditate on God's faithfulness to fulfill God's promises? What promises do you see as not yet completely fulfilled? What part do you have to play in the fulfillment of those promises?

CONCLUSION

A young girl goes about her daily routine in an obscure Galilean village. A priest performs his duties in the Jerusalem Temple. Shepherds keep their sheep in the fields outside of Bethlehem. An aging prophet scans the crowds in the Temple precincts. All are greeted with news of God's appearance. Their lives are all changed by their responses to this news, responses placed into little songs that still beckon the voices of God's faithful.

In his study of these canticles in *The Birth of the Messiah,* Raymond Brown points out that we can read the narrative of Luke 1–2 without the songs.[1] We can follow the narrative flow of the story by skipping the canticles; however, that would be like celebrating Advent and Christmas without music. The songs interrupt the story and cause us to pay more attention to the promises of God's appearing. They halt the flow of action and cause us to ponder, to search for a deeper meaning to the events. The songs invite us to meditate on the surprising coming of God into the lives of these characters.

Brown refers to these canticles as mosaics of Old Testament passages. Each canticle is a composition based on phrases and images that occur across the biblical narrative. Matthew dots his birth narrative with quotes from the prophets. Luke gives us songs that resonate with the praises of Israel.

These songs, placed within Luke's narrative of Jesus' birth, interpret the events in light of God's promises across generations. They appear as compositions based on the characters' pondering God's coming in light of the biblical faith. The ancient promises are then woven together in a new work that speaks of God's appearance in their lives.

Pondering God's appearance to these biblical characters opens up within us the hope, the anticipation, that God will be with us. We are as confident as Mary, singing about God's salvation as a completed action. Like Zechariah, we say—as amazing as God's past and present works are— greater things are coming. We are as enthusiastic as the shepherds wanting to share this news with others. And like Simeon, we are vigilant, scanning our daily events for signs of God's presence.

I have repeatedly referred to these sudden and unexpected visitations as interruptions. But they are not annoying disturbances of the routine; they are welcome reorientations of these lives. They open up new vocations. An unwed girl allows God's promises to be nourished within her. A mute priest sings of God's coming greater blessing. Shepherds become heralds of God's presence. An old prophet holds the fulfillment of God's promises.

Another way we refer to the unexpected and life-changing character of God's coming to us is *grace*. These very different characters from the first two chapters of Luke's Gospel remind us that grace is not confined to a particular class or group of people. There is not a certain place we need to go to encounter God's grace. We may be getting water for our daily chores, at our regular work tasks, or vigilantly scanning the horizon for signs of God's movement. Whenever and wherever grace appears, those who welcome it feel comfort that gives birth to joy.

Grace comes to us all—young, unwed teenage girls; old men; nameless shepherds—and transforms our lives. Magnifying, blessing, glorifying, and departing in God's peace allow us to see signs of God's grace that we might otherwise take for granted or ignore. These acts of praise lift grace to our consciousness in a way that reorients us and causes us to give voice to joyful songs of God's comforting presence with us.

LEADER'S GUIDE

This study can be used in a small-group format. I recommend covering one section or canticle per week, creating a four-week study. The following is a suggested format for each week. I encourage not only reading the canticle but also listening to musical settings and viewing artwork based on the characters singing the canticles. You could vary the order of the group reading, listening, or examining artwork. If you rotate facilitators week to week, the order could be altered by each facilitator. You could also assign various members to take responsibility for one of these parts of the group meeting. For example, if you have members who are gifted in music, they might prefer to choose the musical selection(s) to play for the group. Someone with a strong interest in art could take responsibility for choosing works of art for the group to view.

Sessions are planned for one hour. To allow plenty of participation and sharing, groups of eight to twelve are best. If the group is larger than this, you may want to divide into smaller groups to discuss some of the material. If you are meeting in person, arrange chairs so participants are facing one another, whether using tables or open seating. You may want to use a TV or large computer monitor to show images of artwork or play musical performances of the canticles. Depending on the group makeup or time constraints, you might add an additional session to discuss the overall format and the introduction to the book. Have a time of introductions and let people share why they are interested in this study. Ask participants how they react when they first start to hear Christmas music each season. Let members share some of their favorite Advent and Christmas music. If you need to keep to a four-week format, some of this could be added in a shortened format to the first session.

Session Format

Gather (3–5 minutes): Encourage members to greet one another. Remind everyone that verbal participation is not required. Invite participants to share at whatever level they feel comfortable. You might light a candle to represent the gathering of the group.

Opening Prayer (2–3 minutes): This could be a group prayer said in unison, based on the canticle for the week, or an extemporaneous prayer calling the presence of the Spirit into your gathering. Do what is comfortable for your group, but do not fear experimenting or introducing a prayer practice. Members may be more willing to try something new in a short-term group.

Read the Canticle (2–3 minutes): You could have a designated member read the canticle or read in unison as a group. You could choose a particular translation of the canticle to have all the member use during the week and read that together when you gather to discuss the canticle.

Seeing the Word (15 minutes): Show on a TV or monitor images of some artwork based on the context of the canticle. Share why this artist's rendition was important to share with the group. Share how the painting highlights certain emotions or brings parts of the text to your attention. Allow others to share their observations or other works of art they may have found helpful in interpreting the text.

Hearing the Word (15 minutes): Play a recording of one of the musical settings of the canticle. How does the composition help you focus on certain parts of the text? Consider whether the mood of the music matches the mood you imagine when you read the text. Let others share what they learned from other musical settings. If time allows, play a couple of different arrangements.

Sharing the Text (15 minutes): Allow members to share things they have learned or practiced or questions they might have based on the reading for the week. You could choose a few questions from each section to have ready in case participants need some prompting to get started with this sharing.

Praying for One Another (10 minutes): Invite members to share joys or concerns that they would like to include in prayers. Members could pray for each other in groups of two, or a prayer could be offered by one member for the whole group. Some groups prefer to close by allowing each member to offer a brief prayer. Your group could alternate formats for each closing session.

NOTES

Introduction

1. Charles Dickens, *A Christmas Carol* (New York: Fall River Press, 2013), 11.

Section One: Mary's Song—The *Magnificat*

1. Robert Tannehill has written an extended study of the poetic effect of the *Magnificat*. See "The Magnificat as Poem," *Journal of Biblical Literature*, 263–75.

Section Three: The Angels' Song—The *Gloria in Excelsis*

1. For more information on pronunciation battles, see James Harbeck, "How do you prounounce 'in excelsis'?" The Week, December 21, 2016, https://theweek.com/articles/666146/how-pronounce-excelsis.
2. Verlyn D. Verbrugge, "The Heavenly Army on the Fields of Bethlehem (Luke 2:13-14)," *Calvin Theological Journal* 42, no. 2 (2008): 301–11.

Conclusion

1. Raymond E. Brown, S. S., *The Birth of the Messiah: A Commentary on the Infancy Narratives in Matthew and Luke* (New York: Image, 1979), 346–55.

BIBLIOGRAPHY

Borg, Marcus, J. and John Dominic Crossan. *The First Christmas.* New York: HarperOne, 2007.

Boyce, James L. "For You Today a Savior: The Lukan Infancy Narrative." *Word and World* 27, no. 4 (Fall 2007): 371–80.

Brown, Raymond E. *The Birth of The Messiah.* New York: Doubleday, 1977.

Dennison, James T. "Simeon's Farwell Song." *Kerux* 16, no. 3 (December 2001): 10–17.

Dickens, Charles. *A Christmas Carol.* New York: Fall River Press, 2013.

Foster, Ruth Ann. "Mary's Hymn of Praise in Luke 1:46b-55: Reflection on Liturgy and Spiritual Formation." *Review and Expositor* 100 (Summer 2003): 451–63.

Martindale, C. C. "The Benedictus Canticle." *Worship* 30, no.1 (December 1955): 42–44.

—— "The Magnificat." *Worship* 30, no. 2 (January 1956): 140–42.

—— "Simeon's Canticle." *Worship* 30, no. 3 (February 1956): 199–201.

Meyer, Ben F. "But Mary Kept All These Things. . ." *The Catholic Biblical Quarterly* 26. no. 1 (January 1964): 31–49.

Stohlman, David H. "Hymns for the New Age." *Currents in Theology and Mission* 8, no. 6 (December 1981): 366–69.

Tannehill, Robert C. "The Magnificat As Poem." *Journal of Biblical Literature* 93, no. 2 (June 1974): 263–75.

Verbrugge, Verlyn D. "The Heavenly Army on the Fields of Bethlehem (Luke 2:13-14)." *Calvin Theological Journal* 43, no. 2 (2008): 301–11.

Witherup, Ronald D., S. S. "Singing for Joy." *The Priest* (December 2012): 10–12.